Land That I Love

THOMAS KINKADE

HARVEST HOUSE PUBLISHERS

EUGENE, OREGON

America! America!

God shed His grace on thee,

And crown thy good with brotherhood

From sea to shining sea.

God Shed His Grace

Katherine Lee Bates

Land That I Love

Text Copyright © 2002 by Media Arts Group, Inc., Morgan Hill,
CA 95037 and Harvest House Publishers, Eugene, OR 97402

ISBN 0-7369-1020-4

Harvest House Publishers has made every effort to trace the ownership
of all poems and quotes in this book. In the event of a question arising
from the use of any poem or quote, we regret any error made and will
be pleased to make the necessary correction in future editions.

Design and production by Koechel Peterson & Associates, Mpls., MN

Printed in the United States

02 03 04 05 06 / IP / 5 4

I hear America singing,
the varied carols I hear,
Those of mechanics, each one singing
his as it should be blithe and strong,
The carpenter singing his as he measures his
plank or beam,

The mason singing his as he makes ready for
work, or leaves off work…
The shoemaker singing as he sits on his bench,
the hatter singing as he stands,
The wood-cutter's song, the ploughboy's on
his way in the morning,
Or at noon intermission or at sundown,
The delicious singing of the mother, or of the
young wife at work,
Or of the girl sewing or washing,
Each singing what belongs to him or her and
to none else.

Walt Whitman

ommunity is a beautiful
thing; sometimes it even
heals us and makes us better
than we would otherwise be.

Philip Gulley

Community

How wonderful it is, how pleasant,
when brothers live in harmony!

The Book of Psalms

Thomas Kinkade

ll the flags were fluttering and everybody was happy, because they were free and independent and this was Independence Day.

Flags Were Fluttering

Laura Ingalls Wilder
FARMER BOY

Nobody knows anything about America
who does not know its little towns.

Dorothy Thompson

This Small Town

nce there was an old and very wise man. Every day he would sit in his rocking chair and wait to greet motorists as they passed though his small town.

A family that was passing through stopped for gas. "Is this town a pretty good place to live?" asked the father. The old man replied, "What about the town you are from?" The father said, "In the town I'm from everyone is very close and willing to lend a helping hand." "You know, that's a lot like this small town," replied the old man.

No matter where you move, you take your own attitude with you and that's what makes it terrible or wonderful.

Excerpted from "What's It Like in Your Town?"
STORIES FOR THE HEART

On Waverly Street, everybody knew everybody else. It was only one short block, after all....The trees were elderly maples with lumpy bulbous trunks. The squat clapboard houses seemed mostly front porch.

Sidewalks and Shade Trees

Highway 163 becomes Main Street— becomes every other small-town Main Street: a long, long street of small clapboard houses, most of them white, with sidewalks and shade trees and porch swings and a letter carrier trudging along with his bag.

Berton Roueché
SPECIAL PLACES

...Number Eight was the Bedloe family. They were never just the Bedloes, but the Bedloe *family*, Waverly Street's version of the ideal, apple-pie household: two amiable parents, three good-looking children, a dog, a cat, a scattering of goldfish.

Anne Tyler
SAINT MAYBE

The Small Church

About half past ten the cracked bell of the small church began to ring, and presently the people began to gather for the morning sermon. The Sunday-school children distributed themselves about the house and occupied pews with their parents, so as to be under supervision. Aunt Polly came, and Tom and Sid and Mary sat with her; Tom being placed next the aisle, in order that he might be as far away from the open window and the seductive outside summer scenes as possible.

Mark Twain
ADVENTURES OF TOM SAWYER

How often have I loiter'd o'er thy green,

Where humble happiness endear'd each scene;

How often have I paus'd on every charm,

The shelter'd cot, the cultivated farm,

Humble Happiness

The never-failing brook, the busy mill,

The decent church that topp'd the neighboring hill,

The hawthorn bush, with seats beneath the shade,

For talking age and whisp'ring lovers made!

Oliver Goldsmith

Mid pleasures and palaces

though we may roam,

Be it ever so humble,

there's no place like home;

A charm from the skies seems

to hallow us there,

Sweet, Sweet Home

Which, seek through the world,

is ne'er met with elsewhere.

Home, home, sweet, sweet home!

There's no place like home!

There's no place like home!

J. H. Payne

Peace be to you, and peace be to your

house, and peace be to all that you have.

THE BOOK OF 1 SAMUEL

he clean, bright, gardened townships spoke of country fare and pleasant summer evenings on the stoop.

Gardened Townships

It was a sort of paradise.

Robert Louis Stevenson

There was also a grocery store, so well-known for its fresh poultry and produce from local sources that most people simply called it The Local. For thirty-six years, The Local had provided chickens,

Under the Green Awnings

rabbits, sausage, hams, butter, cakes, pies, free-range eggs, jams and jellies from a farming community in the valley, along with vegetables and berries in season. In summer, produce bins on the sidewalk under the green awnings were filled each day with Silver Queen corn in the shuck. And in July, pails of fat blackberries were displayed in the cooler case.

Jan Karon
AT HOME IN MITFORD

At one of the windows, a few minutes later, Pollyanna gave a glad cry and clapped her hands joyously. "Oh, Nancy, I hadn't seen this

Shining Just Like Silver

before," she breathed. "Look—way off there, with those trees and the houses and that lovely church spire, and the river shining just like silver. Why, Nancy, there doesn't anybody need any pictures with that to look at."

Eleanor H. Porter
POLLYANNA

Richland Lane was untrafficked, hushed, planted in great shade trees, and peopled by wonderfully collected children.

Those Sweet Years

They were sober, sane, quiet kids, whose older brothers and sisters were away at boarding school or college. Every warm night we played organized games— games that were the sweetest part of those sweet years....

Annie Dillard
AN AMERICAN CHILDHOOD

*J*t is a quiet town, where much of the day you could stand in the middle of Main Street and not be in anyone's way—not forever, but for as long as a person would want to stand in the middle of a street.

A Quiet Town

Garrison Keillor
LAKE WOBEGON DAYS

All hail the tranquil village!

May nothing jar its ease,

Where the spiders build their bridges

From the trolleys to the trees.

Author Unknown

The Tranquil Village

As the streets and lanes gave way to countryside and sloped toward the deeper valley, the rolling farmland began...lakes were filled with trout and brim...and everywhere, in town or out, was the rich black loam that made the earthworm's toil one of unending satisfaction.

Jan Karon
At Home in Mitford

*I*n the small towns of the country, however, we found the hospitality of the residents all that we could desire, and more than we could enjoy.

J. S. Buckingham

More Than We Could Enjoy

Cheerfully share your home with those who need a meal or a place to stay for the night.

THE BOOK OF 1 PETER

When Laura looked up from her work she could see almost the whole town, because nearly all the buildings were in the two blocks across the street.

Almost the Whole Town

All their false fronts stood up, square cornered at different heights, trying to make believe that the buildings were two stories high.

Laura Ingalls Wilder
LITTLE TOWN ON THE PRAIRIE

carlett had always liked Atlanta for the very same reasons that made Savannah, Augusta, and Macon condemn it. Like herself, the town was a mixture of the old and new in

The Old and New

Georgia, in which the old came off second best in its conflicts with the self-willed and vigorous new. Moreover, there was something personal, exciting about a town that was born—or at least christened— the same year she was christened.

Margaret Mitchell
GONE WITH THE WIND

merica! the land we love!

God's second gift from

Heaven above,

The Land We Love

Builded and fashioned out of truth

Sinewed by Him with splendid youth

For that glad day when shall be furled

All tyrant flags throughout the world.

For this, our banner holds the sky:

That liberty shall never die.

For this, America began:

To make a brotherhood of man.

Edgar Guest
AMERICA

here s Main Street . . . why, that s Mr. Morgan s drugstore before he changed it! Oh, that s the town I knew as a little girl. And look,

The Town I Knew

there s the old white fence that used to be around our house. Oh, I d forgotten that! Oh, I love it so!

Thornton Wilder
OUR TOWN

his is a dream as old as America itself: give me a piece of land to call my own, a little town where everyone knows my name.

Faith Popcorn

Everyone Knows My Name

People care about you here. Sometimes even to the point of being nosy. When somebody gets sick or dies, the neighbors all pitch in and help. They bring in food you wouldn't believe—casseroles, cakes, green beans, a ham. There's a pace here that I like. It's so different from the East…just a nice old country town.

Berton Rouché
SPECIAL PLACES

We stayed in the hotel where Dad often sat and talked in the lobby, a big glittering place that awed Mom and me. We had a room I can see now. The carpet went from wall to wall. The furniture was big and shining, with a full-length mirror in the door. There was a bathroom between the rooms, with the first big white bathtub I had ever used.

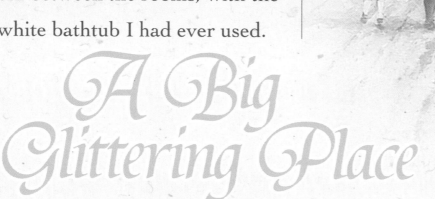

A Big Glittering Place

I couldn't remember a time when Dad had been so gay. He called up and ordered ice water sent up to the room and tipped the boy who brought it, as though he were a king.

Mildred Walker
WINTER WHEAT

Streetcars ran on Penn Avenue. Streetcars were orange, clangy, beloved things—loud, jerky, and old. They were powerless beasts compelled to travel stupidly with their

Beloved Things

wheels stuck in the tracks below them. Each streetcar had one central headlight, which looked fixedly down its tracks and nowhere else.

Annie Dillard
An American Childhood

Paintings

3   Hyde Street and the Bay, San Francisco
4   Village Christmas
5   Carmel—Ocean, Ave.
7   Flags Over the Capitol
10   Hometown Evening
12   Hometown Memories 1
14   Hometown Chapel
16   Lamplight Lane

19   Sunday Outing
20   Lamplight Bridge
22   Carmel—DeLores Street
25   Cobblestone Brook 1
26   Cobblestone Lane
29   Country Memories
30   Hometown Lake
32   Village Inn
35   Placerville, Main Street at Dusk, 1916
36   Main Street Celebration
39   Main Street Courthouse
40   Main Street Matinee
42   Main Street Trolley
45   New York, Snow on 7th
46   San Francisco, Market Street